Thomas Jefferson Murrey

Cookery for Invalids

Thomas Jefferson Murrey

Cookery for Invalids

ISBN/EAN: 9783744789790

Printed in Europe, USA, Canada, Australia, Japan

Cover: Foto ©Lupo / pixelio.de

More available books at **www.hansebooks.com**

FOR

INVALIDS

BY

THOMAS J. MURREY

Author of " Fifty Soups," " Fifty Salads," " Breakfast
Dainties," " Puddings and Dainty Desserts,"
" The Book of Entrées," etc., etc.

NEW YORK
WHITE, STOKES, & ALLEN
1887

CONTENTS.

INTRODUCTORY.

THIS little handbook is offered to house-keepers, in order that they may readily understand the popular dietetic formulas so universally recommended by physicians, many of whom neglect the details of preparing the nutriment they prescribe, owing probably to the fact that all physicians are not cooks, as many of them were in olden, and all of them should be in modern, times.

An exhaustive work on the subject of dietetics would naturally embrace many things, which, while excellent in certain diseases, would lead to distressing results in others. Care should therefore be exercised not to administer other than the most simple diet until the nature of a disease is known, and even then the habits of the invalid should be taken into consideration.

A nurse must always keep in view the fact that the great desideratum is to administer the most nutritious food in such form that the patient can most easily assimilate it.

One word in regard to patent medicines. The sick-room is not the place for experiments, and we trust the time is not far distant when all so-called remedies and alleged health foods and drinks shall not be permitted to be sold or offered for sale, until they receive the indorsement of responsible boards of health.

The lives that are sacrificed yearly by the administration of soothing (?) syrups and other pernicious nostrums are something terrible to contemplate, and the most stringent laws should be in force regulating their sale ; in no case should they be sold without a physician's prescription.

Nurses have been known to purchase these poisonous compounds, and clandestinely administer them to children in their charge, thereby dwarfing their intellects, and, in some instances, actually destroying the lives of the children.

BROTHS.

Beef Broth.—A well-made beef broth contains more nutriment than the old-fashioned beef tea, and is therefore the best of the many nourishing formulas known to the sick-room.

In appearance, also, the broth is far superior to the tea, which is a very important factor in the diet for the sick.

The choicest piece of meat for broth is a neck piece. Chop bone and meat quite small, and see to it that there is about one third bone to two thirds meat. Put into a gallon crock or jar one pound of the meat, and add a quart of cold water; cover the jar with a plate, and place it in a deep saucepan of water. Simmer for four hours, strain into a smaller saucepan, and boil until reduced nearly one half; remove every particle of fat or scum. Now comes the all-important question of seasoning, wherein we are necessarily obliged to consult the fastidious tastes of the invalid. Celery-salt or a stalk of celery allowed to simmer in the broth is acceptable, and the best mode of adding pepper (when it is allowed) is to let a red-pepper pod remain in the broth for a moment or two. Ground pepper is objectionable for various reasons. Dyspeptic patients are very apt to crave seasonings that cannot be taken with impunity. To serve beef broth, care must be exercised that it is not too hot ; half a cupful at a time is all that should be served.

Beef Juice.—Have the dealer cut a thin slice of rump steak, remove the fat, and singe the outside slightly, then scrape it into shreds with a knife. Warm the beef-press by pouring hot water over it, dry it, and with it press out the juice into glass or cup. Place the cup in warm water, and allow the juice to become quite warm, and add a little salt. A warmed lemon-squeezer may be used instead of the press.

Rump steak is recommended because it contains more flavor than other cuts.

Beef Tea for Convalescents.—As the old-fashioned beef tea is sometimes recommended, we give the following recipe for its preparation : Shred half a pound of lean steak, let it stand in a pint of cold water for three quarters of an hour, then put both into a quart champagne bottle. Cut a long slit in the cork before placing it in the bottle. Set the bottle in a saucepan of warm water, simmer one hour and a half, and strain through a napkin into a goblet. Now add a teaspoonful of finely shredded raw, lean beef, let stand a few moments, add a little salt and serve.

Liebig's Extract of Beef.—This and other extracts are often recommended by physicians.

A singular fact in connection with this extract is that the extract made in Texas by this firm is, in the opinion of some of our leading physicians, worthless as nutriment, while the extract made in South America, by the same company, is highly recommended.

The author, being somewhat surprised that there should be a difference, made inquiries and learned that to the flesh of every two *vacá* (fat cow) was added a third of the flesh of a *segua*, or mare, in making the extract. These animals feed on esportillo, which is a thin, reed-like grass, said to be very fattening. The extract made in the United States is prepared from beef only.

Is there more nutriment in the flesh of the horse than in that of the cow?

Mutton Broth.—Although mutton possesses a lower degree of nutritive value than beef, it is nevertheless one of the most important of animal foods, being easily digested.

Like beef, the neck part of mutton is most

appropriate for the making of broth.   Trim off
the surplus fat from the piece of meat, and to a
pound of the lean (with bone added) add a
quart of cold water ; simmer gently for two hours,
strain, and let it become cold.   When wanted
remove every particle of fat.   Put a small quantity of it in a saucepan, and allow it to become
quite hot ; salt slightly, and allow a red-pepper
pod to remain in it for a moment.   Have ready
a small quantity of boiled rice, add it to the
broth, and let stand a few moments before serv-
ing.   A very small piece of onion is sometimes
added to the meat when first cooked to destroy
the peculiar mutton flavor which is so objectionable to many patients.

Veal Broth.—Veal, although less nutritive
than either beef or mutton, and less digestive, is
sometimes recommended, owing to its having a
laxative action.   The broth is prepared in a
similar way to mutton broth.

Chicken Broth.—'' The domestic chicken,''
says Barthalow, '' is a most important article of
food for sick and convalescents.   The taste is
agreeable, the tissues soft and easy of mastica-
tion and digestion.   Spring chickens are more
tender and delicate than the fully developed
fowls of four to six months old.   Next to the
chicken in point of digestibility is the domestic

turkey, and after this the domestic goose and duck." Cut up half a chicken into neat pieces ; add a quart of cold water and a small piece of celery ; cover and boil slowly for two hours. Then remove all fat carefully, strain, add salt, and serve. If rice is used, boil it with the chicken, and add it half an hour before the chicken is cooked.

Scallop Broth.—The peculiar flavor of scallops is quite atrractive to the convalescent, and a broth made from them is nourishing ; but care should be exercised in selecting the shell-fish. To improve their appearance, shippers add quantities of salæratus to the scallops, which has the effect of bleaching them and increasing their size ; this custom may please the dealers, but not consumers. Select medium-sized scallops of a natural creamy color, wash them, and cut them into small pieces. To a half a pint of these add half a pint of warm water and half a pint of milk, a " pea" of butter, and a pinch of salt ; simmer for twenty minutes ; strain and serve.

A pint of milk and no water may be used if the patient desires it.

GRUELS.

Oatmeal Gruel. — Oatmeal, in any form, should not be given to patients who are suffering from diarrhœal diseases or of irritable mucous membrane.   While it is rich in nutriment, it is not always a good food, because it is irritating.

Dr. Mott says that while many are under the impression that oatmeal is a true laxative, it is not properly so.   Sift two ounces of oatmeal. Boil a quart and a pint of water, add to it a salt-spoonful of salt ; now add gradually the oatmeal, stirring constantly while adding the meal. Boil for one hour, remove to the back of the range until water enough has evaporated to make it of the proper consistency ; part milk may be used instead of all water.

This recipe calls for the " old process" milling, which requires much longer cooking than the new preparations now on the market, many of which are advertised as being partly cooked, requiring but a few moments' more cooking to convert them into the most excellent food.

Housekeepers, when preparing oatmeal for delicate stomachs, should ignore the ten, or even twenty-minute, propositions, and cook these preparations at least one hour.

Cerealine Gruel.—Proceed as for oatmeal gruel, and add half a pint of cerealine to a quart of boiling water, slightly salted. Boil for half an hour, and serve with a little sugar. All milk may be used, if desired.

Rice Gruel.—Mix together one tablespoonful of rice-floor, a saltspoonful of salt, and a small cup of cold water. Add the contents of the cup to a pint of boiling water, and boil for twenty minutes. Sugar should be served separately, and, when too thick, add milk until of the proper consistency.

Arrow-Root Gruel.—Take one tablespoonful of arrow-root, a pinch of salt, and half a gill of cold water, stir into half a pint of boiling water, and boil for fifteen minutes.

Barley Gruel.—Take two tablespoonfuls of pearl barley washed in warm water. To a quart and half a pint of cold water add a heaping saltspoonful of salt and the washed barley. Boil for three quarters of an hour ; strain ; add a cake of cut sugar to each gobletful, and twist over the glass a piece of lemon-peel, the oil of which gives a pleasant flavor.

Barley Water.—Wash one ounce of pearl barley in cold water. Drain off the water, and add to a quart and a pint of boiling water the barley, a piece of lemon-peel, and sugar enough to be just perceptible to the taste ; simmer on back of range until reduced one half, and serve unstrained. Other harmless flavoring ingredients may be used instead of the lemon.

Rice Water.—To a quart and a pint of cold water add two ounces of well-washed rice ; salt slightly, and add two cakes of sugar. Boil in the double saucepan until the rice has dissolved. Flavor with lemon-peel or stick cinnamon.

A palatable jelly is made by straining the liquid, and flavoring it with lemon, wine, or brandy, then poured into moulds and placed on ice.

Alcohol, in any form, should not be allowed patients except under medical advice.

TOAST.

Toast is very palatable and digestible when properly prepared. Many seem to think that they have made toast when they brown the outside of a slice of bread. Have they?

The object in making toast is to evaporate all moisture from the bread, and holding a slice over the fire to singe does not accomplish this; it only warms the moisture, making the inside of the bread doughy and decidedly indigestible. The true way of preparing it is to cut the bread into slices a quarter of an inch thick, trim off all crust, put the slices in a pan or plate, place them in the oven—which must not be too hot— take them out when a delicate brown, and butter at once.

For my own use I dry all home-made bread in this manner.

Dry Toast should be served within the folds of a napkin if you wish to keep it hot; toast-racks allow the heat to escape, and they are not recommended.

Dip Toast.—Prepare the toast as above directed; dip the edges into hot water quickly, and butter at once. This is also called **water toast.**

Milk Toast.—Wet the pan to be used with cold water, which prevents burning. Melt an ounce of floured butter ; whisk into it a pint of hot milk ; add a little salt ; simmer. Prepare four slices of toast ; put them in a deep dish one at a time ; pour a little of the milk over each, and over the last one pour the remainder of the milk.

Anchovy Toast.—The best way to prepare this appetizing dish is as follows : Toast the bread and trim it neatly, and place it near the range to keep warm ; next prepare a " dip," as for ordinary cream toast ; spread a thin layer of anchovy paste on each slice of bread ; place in a hot, deep dish ; pour the prepared cream over them, and serve.

Clam Toast.—Chop up two dozen small clams into fine pieces ; simmer for thirty minutes in hot water enough to cover them. Beat up the yolks of two eggs ; add a little cayenne and a gill of warmed milk ; dissolve half a teaspoonful of flour in a little cold milk ; simmer all together ; pour over buttered toast, and serve.

Marrow-bone Toast.—Procure two beef shin-bones about six to eight inches long ; cover them with dough, and wrap them in muslin ; pour hot water enough to cover them, and boil for an hour and a half. Remove cloth and dough ; shake or draw out the marrow with a long-handled fork upon slices of hot toast. Add salt, cayenne, and, if convenient, a little chopped celery, and serve.

Oyster Toast.—Select fifteen plump oysters ; chop them fine, and add salt, pepper, and a suspicion of nutmeg. Beat up the yolks of two eggs with a gill of cream ; whisk this into the simmering oysters. When set, pour the whole over slices of buttered toast.

Salmon Toast.—It very often occurs that a can of salmon is not all used at a meal, and yet there is not quite enough for another meal without other dishes or ingredients added to it. Should this occur, mince the salmon, heat, and season it and serve it on toast. A poached egg added to it is quite acceptable.

Tongue Toast.—A very nice dish is prepared from cold boiled or potted tongue. Slice the tongue, and cut each slice into small, fine pieces ; heat it in a pan with a little butter. To prevent burning, moisten with warm water or clear soup ; add salt and pepper ; stir into it two beaten eggs. When set, arrange neatly on toast.

Dainty bits of roast game, fowl, etc., minced, warmed over, and served on toast are excellent.

DIET DRINKS.

Frappé Champagne renders important service in irritable states of the stomach, especially in sea-sickness, vomiting of pregnancy, yellow-fever, cholera morbus, and cholera. To produce *frappé* champagne quickly, proceed as follows : Put into a metal wine-cooler, or any other metal receptacle, a bottle of dry champagne, surround it with alternate layers of rock salt and cracked ice, place the cooler on the *hot* range, and the rapid melting of the ice will solidify the wine in five minutes ; if allowed to remain a longer period the wine will become solid, and refuse to leave its glassy prison.

When we take into consideration the fact that by the old method of revolving the wine in its icy walls, a period of thirty minutes is required to *frappé* it, the above phenomenal method of producing the desired result will be appreciated.

Sparkling wines, as a rule, are more sedative to the stomach, and more intoxicating relatively to their alcoholic strength than still wines.

Sweet champagnes contain a vast quantity of unappropriated sugar. When such wines are used they produce acid fermentation, and acidity with headache quite naturally follows.

Agents of sweet champagnes wear out their vocal chords telling their patrons to serve wines as cold as possible ; in this way the sugar is not easily detected, and a large sale of particular brands is the result. But let me warn my readers who use champagne that a fine dry champagne is almost ruined by the low temperature at which it is usually served at restaurants, receptions, etc. A very cold champagne is a dangerous tipple for even a healthy stomach, especially near bedtime.

Wine Whey.—Boil a pint of sweet milk and add half a gill of sherry. Let it simmer for fifteen minutes, skim off the curd, add a gill of sherry, and remove curd as it rises. Straining may be necessary to remove the curd entirely. Sweeten.

Eggnog.—Scald half a pint of milk ; when cold add one egg well beaten, two teaspoonfuls of sugar, and a tablespoonful of choice brandy. Shake or beat the mixture with a fork. This formula is only intended for invalids, and is not the recipe used in *cafés*.

Sherry and Egg.—Beat up one egg thoroughly, add a teaspoonful of sugar, and a wine glass full of dry sherry.

FRUIT DRINKS.

Currant-Jelly Water. —Dissolve a teaspoonful of currant-jelly in a goblet of cold water, and add one cake of cut sugar.

Currant Water.—Simmer gently for ten minutes a pint of fresh-picked currants in a quart of water, add a heaping tablespoonful of powdered sugar, and, when cold, strain. There is a little economy in adding the sugar after the juice is strained.

" Out upon the nonsense of taking medicine and nostrums during the currant season ! Let it be taught at theological seminaries that the currant is a ' means of grace.' It is a corrective, and that is what average humanity most needs."—*E. P. Roe, in " The Home Acre."*

Apple Water.—Mash two baked apples with a fork, and pour over them a pint of boiling water ; when cool strain and sweeten to taste.

A Glass of Cold Water in the morning before breakfast will, in many persons, produce the same effect as mineral waters.

MILK.

Skimmed Milk.—In cases of intestinal disorders skimmed milk is better than pure milk, and in cases of disease, when fats must be omitted, it is very useful.

The milk should stand twenty-four hours in a cool place, and all the cream which has risen should be carefully skimmed off.

Buttermilk.—The author, who is an inveterate smoker, has for years drank buttermilk before retiring, and during the day whenever it can be obtained. He is convinced that it neutralizes the effects of the nicotine from the tobacco. The *Journal of Health* says : " Buttermilk is excellent for weak or delicate stomachs, and far better as a dinner drink than coffee, tea, or water, and, unlike them, does not retard, but rather aids, digestion. A celebrated physician once said that if every one knew the value of buttermilk as a drink, it would be more freely partaken of by persons who drink so excessively of other beverages ; and, further, compared its effects upon the system to the clearing out of a cook-stove that has been clogged up with ashes that have sifted through, filling up every crevice and crack, saying that the human system is like

the stove, and collects and gathers refuse matter
that can in no way be exterminated from the
system so effectually as by drinking buttermilk.
It is also a specific remedy for indigestion,
soothes and quiets the nerves, and is very som-
nolent to those who are troubled with sleeplessness.

" Every one who values good health should
drink buttermilk every day in warm weather,
and let tea, coffee, and water alone. For the
benefit of those who are not already aware of it,
I may add that in the churning the first process
of digestion is gone through, making it one of
the easiest and quickest of all things to digest.
It makes gastric juice, and contains properties
that readily assimilate with it, with little or no
wear upon the digestive organs."

Milk, pure and simple, is a natural food, and
should enter into the diet of adults as well as
children. Lime-water is usually added to milk
when the acidity of the stomach causes the latter
to be rejected. When lime water is not obtain-
able, the thorough beating of the milk with a
fork will break the oily particles of the milk,
causing it to digest more rapidly.

A large glass of milk should not be given to
children or persons of weak stomachs, for they
are apt to use it immoderately. It should be

drunk in small mouthfuls, and as slowly as possible.

The quaffing of a glass of cold milk on a hot
day, without stopping to take breath, is a very
dangerous proceeding.

———

FRUITS AS FOOD AND MEDICINE.

Of all the fruits with which we are blessed, the
peach is the most delicious and digestible.
There is nothing more palatable, wholesome,
and medicinal than good ripe peaches. They
should be ripe, but not over-ripe and half-
rotten ; and of this kind they may make a part
of either meal, or be eaten between meals ; but
it is better to make them part of the regular
meals.   It is a mistaken idea that no fruit should
be eaten at breakfast.   It would be far better if
our people would eat less bacon and grease at
breakfast and more fruit.   In the morning there
is an acrid state of the secretions, and nothing
is so well calculated to correct this as cooling
sub-acid fruits, such as peaches, apples, etc.
Still, some of us have been taught that eating

fruit before breakfast is highly dangerous. However the idea originated, it is certainly a great error, contrary to both reason and fact.

The apple is one of the best of fruits. Baked or stewed apples will generally agree with the most delicate stomach, and are excellent medicine in many cases of sickness. Green or half-ripe apples stewed and sweetened are pleasant to the taste, cooling, nourishing, and laxative, far superior, in many cases, to the abominable doses of salts and oil usually given in fever and other diseases. Raw apples and dried apples stewed are better for constipation than liver pills.

Oranges are very acceptable to most stomachs, having all the advantages of the acid alluded to ; but the orange juice alone should be taken, rejecting the pulp.

The same may be said of lemons, pomegranates, and all that class. Lemonade is the best drink in fevers, and, when thickened with sugar, is better than syrup of squills and other nauseous medicines in many cases of cough.

Tomatoes act on the liver and bowels, and are much more pleasant and safe than blue pills and " liver regulators." The juice should be used alone, rejecting the skins.

The small seeded fruits, such as blackberries, figs, raspberries, currants, and strawberries, may be classed among the best foods and medicines. The sugar in them is nutritious, the acid is cooling and purifying, and the seeds are laxative.

We would be much the gainers if we would look more to our orchards and gardens for our medicines, and less to our drug-stores. To cure fever or act on the kidneys, no febrifuge or diuretic is superior to watermelon, which may, with very few exceptions, be taken in sickness and health in almost unlimited quantities, not only without injury, but with positive benefit. But in using them, the water or juice should be taken, excluding the pulp, and the melon should be fresh and ripe, but not over-ripe or stale. — *Family Doctor*.

EATING BEFORE SLEEPING.

A general impression prevails that to eat before going to bed is an injurious and altogether an unwise habit. Much depends on the individual habits of persons ; in the case of one accustomed to dine at six o'clock, and whose hour for retiring is nine o'clock, we must admit it would be unwise to partake of food before sleep. On the other hand, the six-o'clock diner, whose hour for retiring is from midnight to 3 A. M., and whose rising hour is from 8 to 11 A. M., *must* eat before going to bed if he wishes to avoid doctors' bills and sleeplessness. The interval between meals is decidedly too long a period for fasting. Empty stomachs have much to do with insomnia and kindred diseases so prevalent among writers and other brain-workers. The languid, half-rested feeling on rising, and the cross, irritable peevishness of many when spoken to about breakfast are other symptoms of altogether too long a period of fasting. The question of what food is the most suitable to eat before going to bed naturally arises. This must be decided by circumstances. One who has spent the evening in dancing or other exercise, naturally requires something more substantial than one who has spent the evening in a quiet manner.

Raw Oysters thoroughly masticated are easily digested, although weak stomachs should avoid condiments with them, and if the oysters are large, the ligament or muscle should be removed.

Oyster Broth, stew, or soup when prepared with milk is acceptable at late suppers ; but the pernicious habit of many late diners of drinking cold ale and beer with cooked oysters, is one which the author strongly deprecates.

Pigs' Feet when boiled until tender, then nicely broiled over a charcoal fire, are quite digestible, and, should Bass's ale be served with them, see to it that it has not been on ice, and is free from all evidence of carbonic-acid gas, which is found in the " white label " bottling of Bass, making this particular brand objectionable for night drinking.

Stewed Tripe with Oysters may be eaten at night, and a glass of very light Moselle wine —either still or sparkling—may be served with it.

Boiled Sweetbreads cut into slices and warmed up in a light sauce, or served on toast *en brochette*, are not apt to prevent sleep, or produce indigestion.

Poached Eggs are easily digested, but the soggy toast usually served with them is something to avoid.

Boiled Calf's Head cut into pieces as large as an oyster, then fried as one would fry doughnuts, and served with a *sauce tartare*, is a favorite night dish of the author, as is also shad-roe stewed in cream.

Cold Roast Beef, mutton, lamb, venison, or poultry, served with a dainty salad of watercress, or escarale, and a glass of generous claret, is not apt to be despised by one who sits up at night writing.

A dainty surprise for the night-worker would be a plate of sandwiches made from thin slices of the breast of a cold roast canvas-back duck. Crisp celery may accompany the dish. Sandwiches made of cold roast beef and venison are very nice.

Hamburg Steak when reduced to a pulp, and served raw, or but slightly singed to give it the appearance of being cooked, is most easily digested. A raw or slightly poached egg may be served with it.

Raw Meat is invariably recommended in cases of debility when an easily digested nutriment is required. A method of treating *diarrhœa*, long practised in Russia, consists in the use of raw meat, beaten in a mortar until all traces of fibre disappear. It is then seasoned to taste, and served in the form of sandwich. Fruit jelly is sometimes added to disguise the flavor of the meat.

Venison Steak cooked in a chafing-dish, or nicely broiled over a *charcoal* fire, is unquestionably one of the best of meats to eat late at night. While it does not possess the same nutritive value found in beef, it is more easily and quickly digested.

MISCELLANEOUS.

My only serious objection to late suppers is that, unless caution is exercised, one is apt to disarrange the stomach by drinking too much cold liquid, thereby preventing the food from digesting. A Welsh rarebit, in itself, is not so terrible a nightmare-producer as it has been often painted ; but when washed down with iced drinks it becomes a leathery mass of the most indigestible character.

Deviled bones, chickens, kidneys, etc., when eaten late at night are apt to convince one who does not possess the digestive powers of an ostrich, that the name " Deviled " is peculiarly appropriate ; in fact, they are dyspepsia-breeding companions to fried oysters, iced tea, and heavy salads.

In conclusion I will state that each individual must be his own adviser as to what should be eaten late at night ; he should know by experience what dishes agree with him, and not rely upon dogmatic health theories, which are at best confusing to the very people they are intended to benefit.

Calf's-foot Jelly.—The trouble and expense of preparing calf's-foot jelly at home is too

great.   It is therefore advisable to purchase it
from the grocer or from caterers.

The Hot-Water Cure.—Much has been
written for and against this new remedial agent,
and, in the opinion of the author, the " fors"
have the best of it.   A goblet of hot water in the
morning is beneficial to those who dine late the
night before.   Care must be exercised that the
water is drawn fresh from the faucet, brought to
boiling point, then served.

Many are apt to serve hot water that has stood
on the range over-night, the effect of which is
one of nausea.

www.ingramcontent.com/pod-product-compliance
Lightning Source LLC
Chambersburg PA
CBHW021457090426
42739CB00009B/1765